YOUR DANIEL FAST JOURNAL

BY SUSAN GREGORY

Author of *The Daniel Fast: feed your soul,*
strengthen your spirit and renew your body

For more help on using this journal,
please visit <u>Daniel-Fast.com/journal</u>

Visit the Daniel Fast website at www.Daniel-Fast.com

The Daniel Fast Journal Copyright © 2018 by Susan Gregory. All rights reserved.

YOUR DANIEL FAST JOURNAL

BY SUSAN GREGORY

Author of *The Daniel Fast: feed your soul,
strengthen your spirit and renew your body*

Publishers

Experience a successful Daniel Fast by using the bestselling book used by hundreds of thousands of believers throughout the world.

In her bestselling book, Susan Gregory shares the secrets for a successful fasting experience. Learn about the ancient spiritual discipline of fasting that God designed for His people. Use the collection of recipes provided for your entire 21-day fast. Plus, feed your soul each day with the daily devotions. The go-to guide has everything you need for a powerful and meaningful fast.

Available wherever books are sold.

Join the Community

Thank you for purchasing Your Daniel Fast Journal. My sincere hope is that this period of extended prayer and fasting will bring you the desires of your heart as you draw nearer to God and develop your faith in Jesus Christ.

A great blessing awaits you as you connect with others who have used the Daniel Fast as their method of spiritual fasting. I also offer ongoing support for your journey in faith with newsletters and Christ-centered coaching programs.

Please be assured that we NEVER share your contact information with anyone for any reason. And we only deliver messages intended to help and support you and others as you grow in the love and knowledge of Jesus.

To subscribe to my free newsletter, visit the Daniel Fast website at www.Daniel-Fast.com

You will also find ways to connect with other like-minded people at the website.

BE BLESSED ON YOUR FAST

Draw near to God and He will draw near to you.
James 4:8

How to use Your Daniel Fast Journal ~

Imagine that you're off on a 21-day personal retreat. You're on an adventure of sorts. A spiritual journey. And to make sure your experience is orderly and pleasant you want to plan your days and also record your intentions and thoughts. That's the purpose for this journal.

Use the journal to **plan your meals**. Keep them simple. And make sure you focus your attention on your spiritual goals and desire rather than on the food.

Take time to consider what you really want for your life now and your future. Record ten of the **desires of your heart** in this journal. Use the pages as worksheets to make your petitions known to God and to follow the instructions Jesus gives believers to follow.

Each morning use Your Daniel Fast Journal as a tool to connect with the Lord, the desire of your heart, and the plans you have for the day.

When you **complete your fast,** reflect on your personal retreat time. Have a "little meeting with yourself" and consider what you've learned about God, His ways, and yourself. What good habits have your adopted? What have you released? And how will you move forward.

You can also use the journal to **make notes** that will help you on your spiritual journey.

Above all, be blessed as you open your heart to the Lord and receive the immeasurable love He has for you.

I hope the very best for you on your fast.

Be blessed,

Susan Gregory

Simple Meals for a Meaningful Fast

Blessed are those who hunger and thirst for righteousness,
for they shall be filled.
Matthew 5:6

The Daniel Fast is a partial fast where some foods are eaten and others are restricted. The fast is based on the fasting experiences of the Old Testament prophet Daniel along with typical Jewish fasting principles. The passages in the Bible that contribute to the Daniel Fast guidelines are:

Prove thy servants, I beseech thee, ten days; and let them give us pulse to eat,
and water to drink.
Daniel 1:12 KJV

Pulse is food grown from seed. So the Daniel Fast is totally plant-based eating. No animal products at all during the fast. Also, the only beverage is water. No tea. No coffee. No soda. Only water.

I ate no pleasant bread, neither came flesh nor wine in my mouth, neither did
I anoint myself at all, till three whole weeks were fulfilled.
Daniel 10:3 KJV

No pleasant bread, along with notes from other translations, leads us to no leavening agents, not sweeteners (natural or artificial), and no deep-fried foods. For the complete Daniel Fast Guidelines, visit Daniel-Fast.com or read more in the bestselling book and guide for this method fasting, *The Daniel Fast – feed your soul, strengthen your spirit and renew your body*. The book is available from all local and online bookstores.

Keep in mind that purpose of fasting is to restrict food for a spiritual purpose. So keep you meals simple. Watch yourself. Are you denying the flesh? Or are you searching for ways to satisfy the flesh and still eat within the Daniel

Fast Guidelines. You can learn a lot about yourself and your faith as you examine your heart and your ways.

Remember what Jesus teaches us in the Word, *"I am the bread of life. He who comes to Me shall never hunger, and he who believes in Me shall never thirst."* John 6:35

Use this section of Your Daniel Fast Journal to plan your simple meals so you can avoid focusing on the food rather than on God. I encourage you to plan your meals each week. Think of ways you can prepare meals in large batches (cook once eat twice).

Collect recipes for the fast using the Daniel Fast book or those found at Daniel-Fast.com. Select recipes for the following meals:

3 breakfast menus

4 lunch menus

7 dinner menus

3 snacks

Keep the recipes together so they're easy to access. Plan your meals. Then venture out on your shopping trip to get all your ingredients. Return home and wash your fruits and vegetables. Slice and dice salad ingredients and store in airtight containers (make salads in minutes for the next several days). Plan how you will prepare the meals, perhaps making two or more recipes at the same time to take advantage of your time in the kitchen.

I like to play music or listen to podcasts during my kitchen time. The whole experience becomes one of joy and spiritual nourishment.

Use the charts in the following pages to plan your meals (consider writing in pencil so you can make changes if necessary). Then each evening, go to the journal pages for your next day of fasting and write in your menus so you are prepared and can plan ahead for any preparation details.

A key to a successful fasting experience is to keep your meals simple. Read Chapter 1 in the Book of Daniel. Imagine the mindset of the prophet as he kept God at the center of all he did and all the choices he made. Enter your fasting experience with a desire to draw near to God and to nourish your heart with His Word.

WEEK ONE MEAL PLANS

Day	Breakfast	Lunch	Dinner	Snack 1	Snack 2
1					
2					
3					
4					
5					
6					
7					

Notes ~

_____

_____

WEEK TWO MEAL PLANS

Day	Breakfast	Lunch	Dinner	Snack 1	Snack 2
1					
2					
3					
4					
5					
6					
7					

Notes ~

_____

_____

WEEK THREE MEAL PLANS

Day	Breakfast	Lunch	Dinner	Snack 1	Snack 2
1					
2					
3					
4					
5					
6					
7					

Notes ~

~ Notes ~

_____
_____
_____
_____
_____
_____
_____
_____
_____
_____
_____
_____
_____
_____
_____
_____
_____
_____
_____
_____
_____
_____
_____
_____
_____
_____
_____
_____

ASK. BELIEVE. RECEIVE.

*Delight yourself also in the Lord, and He shall give you the
desires of your heart.*
Psalm 37:4

During your sacred time of extended prayer and fasting you will spend time with God in prayer, mediation, and worship. As you enter His throne room of grace, bring your needs, desires, and dreams to Him. He wants you to have the desires of your heart.

Delighting in the Lord is a position of submission, humility, love, and devotion. When you put the Lord first and seek His best for your life, you will find yourself asking for blessings that agree with His will and His ways.

Bringing your desires to the Lord is an essential step in receiving His blessings. Align yourself with the Lord, then follow the instructions of Jesus, *"Therefore I say to you, whatever things you ask when you pray, believe that you receive them, and you will have them."* Mark 11:24

Use this section of your Daniel Fast Journal to declare ten desires you have that you will present to the Lord.

- **Desire** ~ Write the request in your own words, being as specific as possible.

- **God's Promise** ~ Search the Scriptures and find God's promise that relates to your desire. Write the verse or passage in the space provided under your request.

- **Petition** ~ Now write your petition (your request) asking the Lord to fulfill His promise. Remember, He is faithful to keep His promises: *Don't worry about anything; instead, pray about everything. Tell God what you need, and thank him for all he has done. Then you will experience God's peace, which exceeds anything we can understand. His peace will guard your hearts and minds as you live in Christ Jesus.* Philippians 4:6-7 NLT

- **Receive and Give Thanks** ~ Next receive. By faith, receive whatever it is you've requested. Note the date that you are receiving what God has promised. Remember, God's ways are not our ways. In the world "we believe it when we see it." However, in God's kingdom we receive because we trust in God and His Word. We believe in Him. And we know whatever we have requested is on it's way into the earth realm. Trust in God. Only believe. And thank God for what He has done.

- **Fulfillment** ~ Then when the promise manifests in the earth realm, note the details including the date and any particulars that are meaningful to you. Use your answered prayers as remembrances to the Lord for His love and faithfulness toward you, His precious child.

What do you desire? What do you want? Seek God. He wants to bless you. And remember, *"You do not have because you do not ask."* James 4:2

Take your time and think about those things you really want. Then go to your Father, using the instructions from His Word to receive from Him.

Desire 1 ~ _____

_____

_____

_____

God's Promise ~ _____

_____

_____

_____

Petition ~ _____

_____

_____

_____

Receive and Give Thanks ~ _____

_____

_____

_____

Fulfillment ~ _____

_____

_____

_____

Desire 2 ~ _____

_____

_____

_____

God's Promise ~ _____

_____

_____

_____

Petition ~ _____

_____

_____

_____

Receive and Give Thanks ~ _____

_____

_____

_____

Fulfillment ~ _____

_____

_____

_____

Desire 3 ~ _____

_____

_____

_____

God's Promise ~ _____

_____

_____

_____

Petition ~ _____

_____

_____

_____

Receive and Give Thanks ~ _____

_____

_____

_____

Fulfillment ~ _____

_____

_____

_____

Desire 4 ~ _____

_____

_____

_____

God's Promise ~ _____

_____

_____

_____

Petition ~ _____

_____

_____

_____

Receive and Give Thanks ~ _____

_____

_____

_____

Fulfillment ~ _____

_____

_____

_____

Desire 5 ~ _____

_____

_____

_____

God's Promise ~ _____

_____

_____

_____

Petition ~ _____

_____

_____

_____

Receive and Give Thanks ~ _____

_____

_____

_____

Fulfillment ~ _____

_____

_____

_____

Desire 6 ~ _____

_____

_____

_____

God's Promise ~ _____

_____

_____

_____

Petition ~ _____

_____

_____

_____

Receive and Give Thanks ~ _____

_____

_____

_____

Fulfillment ~ _____

_____

_____

_____

Desire 7 ~ _____

_____

_____

_____

God's Promise ~ _____

_____

_____

_____

Petition ~ _____

_____

_____

_____

Receive and Give Thanks ~ _____

_____

_____

_____

Fulfillment ~ _____

_____

_____

_____

Desire 8 ~ _____

_____

_____

_____

God's Promise ~ _____

_____

_____

_____

Petition ~ _____

_____

_____

_____

Receive and Give Thanks ~ _____

_____

_____

_____

Fulfillment ~ _____

_____

_____

_____

Desire 9 ~ _____

_____

_____

_____

God's Promise ~ _____

_____

_____

_____

Petition ~ _____

_____

_____

_____

Receive and Give Thanks ~ _____

_____

_____

_____

Fulfillment ~ _____

_____

_____

_____

Desire 10 ~ _____

_____

_____

_____

God's Promise ~ _____

_____

_____

_____

Petition ~ _____

_____

_____

_____

Receive and Give Thanks ~ _____

_____

_____

_____

Fulfillment ~ _____

_____

_____

_____

Notes ~

21 Days of Prayer and Fasting

Be anxious for nothing, but in everything by prayer and supplication, with thanksgiving, let your requests be made known to God.
Philippians 4:6

Each morning set your mind and heart on the ways of God. Use the pages in this section to be mindful of those petitions you have set before the Lord. Each day, write them down, and give God thanks for working on your behalf. Remember, you're not asking Him again because you've already received. However, you do what to keep your blessings at the forefront of your mind.

As you list your desires each day, it's very likely that you will have thoughts about more details or actions you can take related to the request. Listen for that still small voice of God as He speaks to you. Follow His promptings. Obey any instructions He speaks to your spirit. Note under each item on your list whatever you may hear from the Lord.

Meditate on God's Truth ~ Slowly read the *Verse of the Day* found at the top of the page. Allow the Holy Spirit to minister to you through God's Word. And then write down what the Lord is saying to you through His written Word.

Focus Your Day ~ Use the next prompts to set your intentions for the day. Prayerfully write your thoughts and continue to seek the Lord's voice as He speaks to your spirit as you meet with Him.

Meals for the Day ~ Use this section to log the simple Daniel Fast meals you have planned for the day. If any preparation is needed, make plans in the morning so you are free from any stresses about what you will organize so that your body is nourished.

Prayer and Notes ~ You'll also find space to write prayers, thanksgivings, and notes.

Day One

Day:_____

Date: _____/_____/_____

Desire 1 _____
_____

Desire 2 _____
_____

Desire 3 _____
_____

Desire 4 _____
_____

Desire 5 _____
_____

Desire 6 _____
_____

Desire 7 _____
_____

Desire 8 _____
_____

Desire 9 _____
_____

Desire 10 _____
_____

Prayer ~ _____
_____

Delight yourself also in the Lord, and He shall give you the desires of your heart.
Psalm 37:4

Lord, I hear this from You ~ _____

_____

Today I give You thanks for ~ _____

_____

I will be a blessing today by ~ _____

_____

I will feed my soul today by ~ _____

_____

Today's Daniel Fast Meals

Breakfast:_____

Lunch: _____

Dinner: _____

Snack 1: _____

Snack 2: _____

Notes:_____

_____

_____

Day Two

Day:_____

Date: _____/_____/_____

Desire 1 _____

_____

Desire 2 _____

_____

Desire 3 _____

_____

Desire 4 _____

_____

Desire 5 _____

_____

Desire 6 _____

_____

Desire 7 _____

_____

Desire 8 _____

_____

Desire 9 _____

_____

Desire 10 _____

_____

Prayer ~ _____

_____

But Jesus looked at them and said, "With men it is impossible, but not with God; for with God all things are possible."
Mark 10:27

Lord, I hear this from You ~ _____

_____

Today I give You thanks for ~ _____

_____

I will be a blessing today by ~ _____

_____

I will feed my soul today by ~ _____

_____

Today's Daniel Fast Meals

Breakfast:_____

Lunch: _____

Dinner: _____

Snack 1: _____

Snack 2: _____

Notes:_____

_____

_____

Day Three

Day:_____

Date: _____/_____/_____

Desire 1 _____

_____

Desire 2 _____

_____

Desire 3 _____

_____

Desire 4 _____

_____

Desire 5 _____

_____

Desire 6 _____

_____

Desire 7 _____

_____

Desire 8 _____

_____

Desire 9 _____

_____

Desire 10 _____

_____

Prayer ~ _____

_____

If then you were raised with Christ, seek those things which are above, where Christ is, sitting at the right hand of God.
Colossians 3:1

Lord, I hear this from You ~ _____

_____

Today I give You thanks for ~ _____

_____

I will be a blessing today by ~ _____

_____

I will feed my soul today by ~ _____

_____

Today's Daniel Fast Meals

Breakfast:_____

Lunch: _____

Dinner: _____

Snack 1: _____

Snack 2: _____

Notes:_____

_____

_____

Day Four

Day:_____

Date: _____/_____/_____

Desire 1 _____

_____

Desire 2 _____

_____

Desire 3 _____

_____

Desire 4 _____

_____

Desire 5 _____

_____

Desire 6 _____

_____

Desire 7 _____

_____

Desire 8 _____

_____

Desire 9 _____

_____

Desire 10 _____

_____

Prayer ~ _____

_____

And God is able to make all grace abound toward you, that you, always having
all sufficiency in all things, may have an abundance for every good work.
2 Corinthians 9:8

Lord, I hear this from You ~ _____

_____

Today I give You thanks for ~ _____

_____

I will be a blessing today by ~ _____

_____

I will feed my soul today by ~ _____

_____

Today's Daniel Fast Meals

Breakfast:_____

Lunch: _____

Dinner: _____

Snack 1: _____

Snack 2: _____

Notes:_____

_____

_____

Day Five

Day:_____

Date: _____/_____/_____

Desire 1 _____
_____

Desire 2 _____
_____

Desire 3 _____
_____

Desire 4 _____
_____

Desire 5 _____
_____

Desire 6 _____
_____

Desire 7 _____
_____

Desire 8 _____
_____

Desire 9 _____
_____

Desire 10 _____
_____

Prayer ~ _____
_____

And whatever things you ask in prayer, believing, you will receive.
Matthew 21:22

Lord, I hear this from You ~ _____

_____

Today I give You thanks for ~ _____

_____

I will be a blessing today by ~ _____

_____

I will feed my soul today by ~ _____

_____

Today's Daniel Fast Meals

Breakfast:_____

Lunch: _____

Dinner: _____

Snack 1: _____

Snack 2: _____

Notes:_____

_____

_____

Day Six

Day:_____

Date: _____/_____/_____

Desire 1 _____

_____

Desire 2 _____

_____

Desire 3 _____

_____

Desire 4 _____

_____

Desire 5 _____

_____

Desire 6 _____

_____

Desire 7 _____

_____

Desire 8 _____

_____

Desire 9 _____

_____

Desire 10 _____

_____

Prayer ~ _____

_____

And you shall remember the Lord your God, for it is He who gives you power to get wealth, that He may establish His covenant which He swore to your fathers, as it is this day.

Deuteronomy 8:18

Lord, I hear this from You ~ _____

_____

Today I give You thanks for ~ _____

_____

I will be a blessing today by ~ _____

_____

I will feed my soul today by ~ _____

_____

Today's Daniel Fast Meals

Breakfast:_____

Lunch: _____

Dinner: _____

Snack 1: _____

Snack 2: _____

Notes:_____

_____

_____

Day Seven

Day:_____

Date: _____/_____/_____

Desire 1 _____

_____

Desire 2 _____

_____

Desire 3 _____

_____

Desire 4 _____

_____

Desire 5 _____

_____

Desire 6 _____

_____

Desire 7 _____

_____

Desire 8 _____

_____

Desire 9 _____

_____

Desire 10 _____

_____

Prayer ~ _____

_____

Be anxious for nothing, but in everything by prayer and supplication, with
thanksgiving, let your requests be made known to God.
Philippians 4:6

Lord, I hear this from You ~ _____

_____

Today I give You thanks for ~ _____

_____

I will be a blessing today by ~ _____

_____

I will feed my soul today by ~ _____

_____

Today's Daniel Fast Meals

Breakfast:_____

Lunch: _____

Dinner: _____

Snack 1: _____

Snack 2: _____

Notes:_____

_____

_____

Day Eight

Day:_____

Date: _____/_____/_____

Desire 1 _____

_____

Desire 2 _____

_____

Desire 3 _____

_____

Desire 4 _____

_____

Desire 5 _____

_____

Desire 6 _____

_____

Desire 7 _____

_____

Desire 8 _____

_____

Desire 9 _____

_____

Desire 10 _____

_____

Prayer ~ _____

_____

But the natural man does not receive the things of the Spirit of God, for they are foolishness to him; nor can he know them, because they are spiritually discerned.
2 Corinthians 2:14

Lord, I hear this from You ~ _____

_____

Today I give You thanks for ~ _____

_____

I will be a blessing today by ~ _____

_____

I will feed my soul today by ~ _____

_____

Today's Daniel Fast Meals

Breakfast:_____

Lunch: _____

Dinner: _____

Snack 1: _____

Snack 2: _____

Notes:_____

_____

_____

Day Nine

Day:_____

Date: _____/_____/_____

Desire 1 _____

_____

Desire 2 _____

_____

Desire 3 _____

_____

Desire 4 _____

_____

Desire 5 _____

_____

Desire 6 _____

_____

Desire 7 _____

_____

Desire 8 _____

_____

Desire 9 _____

_____

Desire 10 _____

_____

Prayer ~ _____

_____

But without faith it is impossible to please Him, for he who comes to God must believe that He is, and that He is a rewarder of those who diligently seek Him.
Hebrews 11:6

Lord, I hear this from You ~ _____

_____

Today I give You thanks for ~ _____

_____

I will be a blessing today by ~ _____

_____

I will feed my soul today by ~ _____

_____

Today's Daniel Fast Meals

Breakfast:_____

Lunch: _____

Dinner: _____

Snack 1: _____

Snack 2: _____

Notes:_____

_____

_____

Day Ten

Day:_____

Date: _____/_____/_____

Desire 1 _____

_____

Desire 2 _____

_____

Desire 3 _____

_____

Desire 4 _____

_____

Desire 5 _____

_____

Desire 6 _____

_____

Desire 7 _____

_____

Desire 8 _____

_____

Desire 9 _____

_____

Desire 10 _____

_____

Prayer ~ _____

_____

Come to Me, all you who labor and are heavy laden, and I will give you rest.
Matthew 11:28

Lord, I hear this from You ~ _____

_____

Today I give You thanks for ~ _____

_____

I will be a blessing today by ~ _____

_____

I will feed my soul today by ~ _____

_____

Today's Daniel Fast Meals

Breakfast:_____

Lunch: _____

Dinner: _____

Snack 1: _____

Snack 2: _____

Notes:_____

_____

_____

Day Eleven

Day:_____

Date: _____/_____/_____

Desire 1 _____
_____

Desire 2 _____
_____

Desire 3 _____
_____

Desire 4 _____
_____

Desire 5 _____
_____

Desire 6 _____
_____

Desire 7 _____
_____

Desire 8 _____
_____

Desire 9 _____
_____

Desire 10 _____
_____

Prayer ~ _____
_____

Fear not, for I am with you; be not dismayed, for I am your God. I will strengthen you, yes, I will help you, I will uphold you with My righteous right hand.

Isaiah 41:10

Lord, I hear this from You ~ _____

_____

Today I give You thanks for ~ _____

_____

I will be a blessing today by ~ _____

_____

I will feed my soul today by ~ _____

_____

Today's Daniel Fast Meals

Breakfast:_____

Lunch: _____

Dinner: _____

Snack 1: _____

Snack 2: _____

Notes:_____

_____

_____

Day Twelve

Day:_____

Date: _____/_____/_____

Desire 1 _____

_____

Desire 2 _____

_____

Desire 3 _____

_____

Desire 4 _____

_____

Desire 5 _____

_____

Desire 6 _____

_____

Desire 7 _____

_____

Desire 8 _____

_____

Desire 9 _____

_____

Desire 10 _____

_____

Prayer ~ _____

_____

Give, and it will be given to you: good measure, pressed down, shaken to-gether, and running over will be put into your bosom. For with the same meas-ure that you use, it will be measured back to you.

Luke 6:38

Lord, I hear this from You ~ _____

_____

Today I give You thanks for ~ _____

_____

I will be a blessing today by ~ _____

_____

I will feed my soul today by ~ _____

_____

Today's Daniel Fast Meals

Breakfast:_____

Lunch: _____

Dinner: _____

Snack 1: _____

Snack 2: _____

Notes:_____

_____

_____

Day Thirteen

Day:_____

Date: _____/_____/_____

Desire 1 _____
_____

Desire 2 _____
_____

Desire 3 _____
_____

Desire 4 _____
_____

Desire 5 _____
_____

Desire 6 _____
_____

Desire 7 _____
_____

Desire 8 _____
_____

Desire 9 _____
_____

Desire 10 _____
_____

Prayer ~ _____
_____

God is our refuge and strength, a very present help in trouble.
Psalm 46:1

Lord, I hear this from You ~ _____

_____

Today I give You thanks for ~ _____

_____

I will be a blessing today by ~ _____

_____

I will feed my soul today by ~ _____

_____

Today's Daniel Fast Meals

Breakfast:_____

Lunch: _____

Dinner: _____

Snack 1: _____

Snack 2: _____

Notes:_____

_____

_____

Day Fourteen

Day:_____

Date: _____/_____/_____

Desire 1 _____

_____

Desire 2 _____

_____

Desire 3 _____

_____

Desire 4 _____

_____

Desire 5 _____

_____

Desire 6 _____

_____

Desire 7 _____

_____

Desire 8 _____

_____

Desire 9 _____

_____

Desire 10 _____

_____

Prayer ~ _____

_____

I have set the Lord always before me; because He is at my right hand I shall not be moved.
Psalm 16:8

Lord, I hear this from You ~ _____

_____

Today I give You thanks for ~ _____

_____

I will be a blessing today by ~ _____

_____

I will feed my soul today by ~ _____

_____

Today's Daniel Fast Meals

Breakfast:_____

Lunch: _____

Dinner: _____

Snack 1: _____

Snack 2: _____

Notes:_____

_____

_____

Day Fifteen

Day:_____

Date: _____/_____/_____

Desire 1 _____

_____

Desire 2 _____

_____

Desire 3 _____

_____

Desire 4 _____

_____

Desire 5 _____

_____

Desire 6 _____

_____

Desire 7 _____

_____

Desire 8 _____

_____

Desire 9 _____

_____

Desire 10 _____

_____

Prayer ~ _____

_____

Now faith is the substance of things hoped for, the evidence of things not seen.
Hebrews 11:1

Lord, I hear this from You ~ _____

_____

Today I give You thanks for ~ _____

_____

I will be a blessing today by ~ _____

_____

I will feed my soul today by ~ _____

_____

Today's Daniel Fast Meals

Breakfast:_____

Lunch: _____

Dinner: _____

Snack 1: _____

Snack 2: _____

Notes:_____

_____

_____

Day Sixteen

Day:_____

Date: _____/_____/_____

Desire 1 _____

_____

Desire 2 _____

_____

Desire 3 _____

_____

Desire 4 _____

_____

Desire 5 _____

_____

Desire 6 _____

_____

Desire 7 _____

_____

Desire 8 _____

_____

Desire 9 _____

_____

Desire 10 _____

_____

Prayer ~ _____

_____

So then faith comes by hearing, and hearing by the word of God.
Romans 10:17

Lord, I hear this from You ~ _____

_____

Today I give You thanks for ~ _____

_____

I will be a blessing today by ~ _____

_____

I will feed my soul today by ~ _____

_____

Today's Daniel Fast Meals

Breakfast:_____

Lunch: _____

Dinner: _____

Snack 1: _____

Snack 2: _____

Notes:_____

_____

_____

Day Seventeen

Date: _____/_____/_____

Desire 1 _____

_____

Desire 2 _____

_____

Desire 3 _____

_____

Desire 4 _____

_____

Desire 5 _____

_____

Desire 6 _____

_____

Desire 7 _____

_____

Desire 8 _____

_____

Desire 9 _____

_____

Desire 10 _____

_____

Prayer ~ _____

_____

This Book of the Law shall not depart from your mouth, but you shall meditate in it day and night, that you may observe to do according to all that is written in it. For then you will make your way prosperous, and then you will have good success.

Joshua 1:8

Lord, I hear this from You ~ _____

_____

Today I give You thanks for ~ _____

_____

I will be a blessing today by ~ _____

_____

I will feed my soul today by ~ _____

_____

Today's Daniel Fast Meals

Breakfast:_____

Lunch: _____

Dinner: _____

Snack 1: _____

Snack 2: _____

Notes:_____

_____

_____

Day Eighteen

Day:_____

Date: _____/_____/_____

Desire 1 _____

_____

Desire 2 _____

_____

Desire 3 _____

_____

Desire 4 _____

_____

Desire 5 _____

_____

Desire 6 _____

_____

Desire 7 _____

_____

Desire 8 _____

_____

Desire 9 _____

_____

Desire 10 _____

_____

Prayer ~ _____

_____

Trust in the Lord with all your heart, and lean not on your own understanding;
in all your ways acknowledge Him, and He shall direct your paths.
Proverbs 3:5-6

Lord, I hear this from You ~ _____

_____

Today I give You thanks for ~ _____

_____

I will be a blessing today by ~ _____

_____

I will feed my soul today by ~ _____

_____

Today's Daniel Fast Meals

Breakfast:_____

Lunch: _____

Dinner: _____

Snack 1: _____

Snack 2: _____

Notes:_____

_____

_____

Day Nineteen

Day:_____

Date: _____/_____/_____

Desire 1 _____

_____

Desire 2 _____

_____

Desire 3 _____

_____

Desire 4 _____

_____

Desire 5 _____

_____

Desire 6 _____

_____

Desire 7 _____

_____

Desire 8 _____

_____

Desire 9 _____

_____

Desire 10 _____

_____

Prayer ~ _____

_____

Trust in the Lord, and do good; dwell in the land, and feed on His faithful-
ness.
Psalm 37:3

Lord, I hear this from You ~ _____

_____

Today I give You thanks for ~ _____

_____

I will be a blessing today by ~ _____

_____

I will feed my soul today by ~ _____

_____

Today's Daniel Fast Meals

Breakfast:_____

Lunch: _____

Dinner: _____

Snack 1: _____

Snack 2: _____

Notes:_____

_____

_____

Day Twenty

Day:_____

Date: _____/_____/_____

Desire 1 _____
_____

Desire 2 _____
_____

Desire 3 _____
_____

Desire 4 _____
_____

Desire 5 _____
_____

Desire 6 _____
_____

Desire 7 _____
_____

Desire 8 _____
_____

Desire 9 _____
_____

Desire 10 _____
_____

Prayer ~ _____
_____

He who does not love does not know God, for God is love.
1 John 4:8

Lord, I hear this from You ~ _____

_____

Today I give You thanks for ~ _____

_____

I will be a blessing today by ~ _____

_____

I will feed my soul today by ~ _____

_____

Today's Daniel Fast Meals

Breakfast:_____

Lunch: _____

Dinner: _____

Snack 1: _____

Snack 2: _____

Notes:_____

_____

_____

Day Twenty-One

Day:_____

Date: _____/_____/_____

Desire 1 _____

_____

Desire 2 _____

_____

Desire 3 _____

_____

Desire 4 _____

_____

Desire 5 _____

_____

Desire 6 _____

_____

Desire 7 _____

_____

Desire 8 _____

_____

Desire 9 _____

_____

Desire 10 _____

_____

Prayer ~ _____

_____

But as it is written: "Eye has not seen, nor ear heard, Nor have entered into the heart of man The things which God has prepared for those who love Him."
1 Corinthians 2:9

Lord, I hear this from You ~ _____

_____

Today I give You thanks for ~ _____

_____

I will be a blessing today by ~ _____

_____

I will feed my soul today by ~ _____

_____

Today's Daniel Fast Meals

Breakfast:_____

Lunch: _____

Dinner: _____

Snack 1: _____

Snack 2: _____

Notes:_____

_____

_____

Concluding Your Daniel Fast

The Lord is my shepherd; I shall not want. He makes me to lie down in green pastures; He leads me beside the still waters. He restores my soul; He leads me in the paths of righteousness for His name's sake.
Psalm 23:1-3

The Daniel Fast is a partial fast where some foods are eaten and others are restricted. The fast is based on the fasting experiences of the Old Testament prophet Daniel along with typical Jewish fasting principles. The passages in the Bible that contribute to the Daniel Fast guidelines are:

What I learned during my fast ~ _____

_____

_____

_____

Habits I will continue in my daily life ~ _____

_____

_____

_____

What I will do better next time ~ _____

_____

_____

_____

What I learned on my fast ~ _____

_____

_____

_____

Notes ~ _____

_____

_____

_____

_____

_____

_____

_____

_____

_____

_____

_____

_____

_____

_____

_____

_____

_____

_____

_____

_____

Made in the USA
Columbia, SC
08 February 2020